Animal Shelter

Why Not Eddie?

Barbara Titus

Illustrated by:
Debra Green

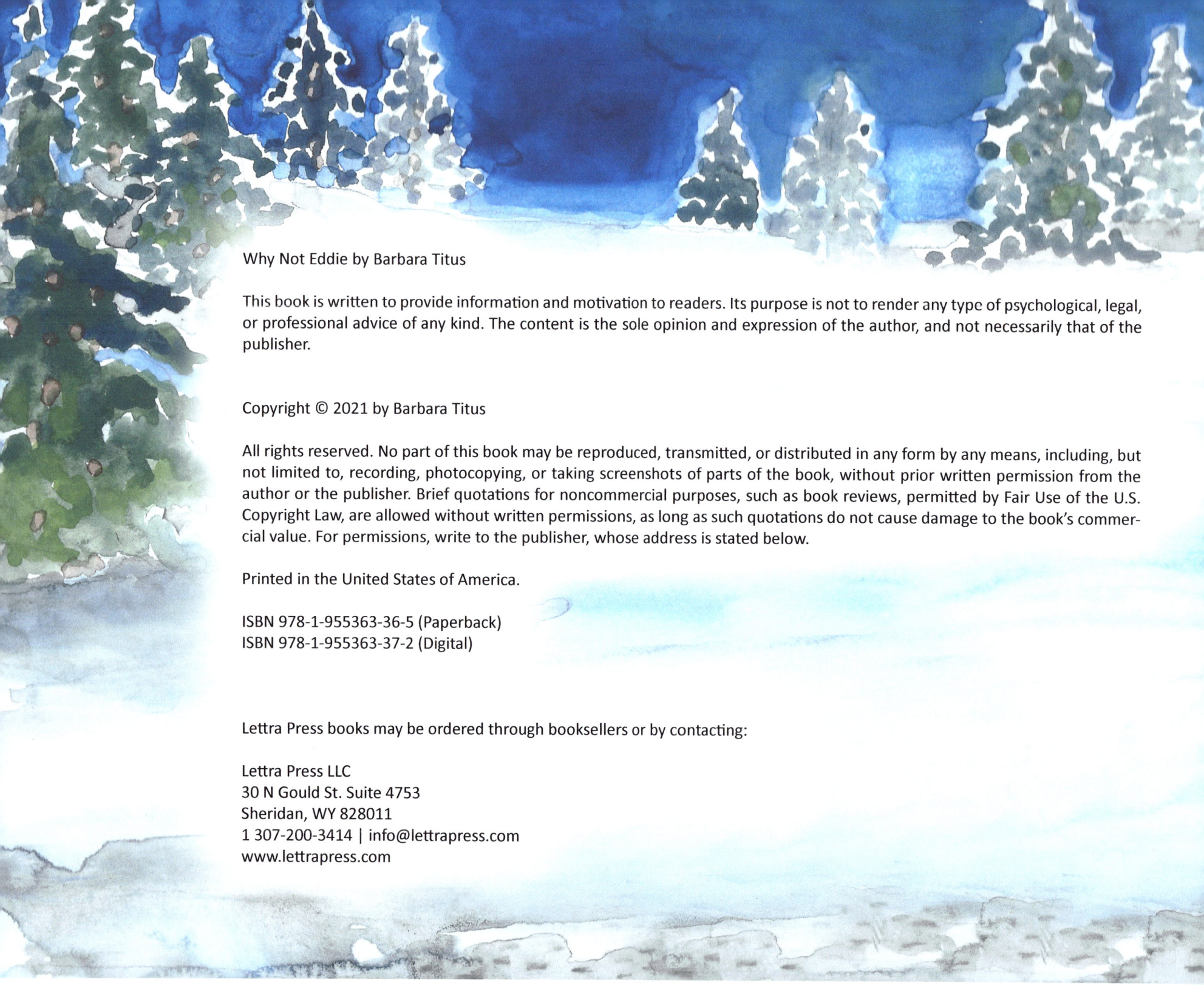

Why Not Eddie by Barbara Titus

This book is written to provide information and motivation to readers. Its purpose is not to render any type of psychological, legal, or professional advice of any kind. The content is the sole opinion and expression of the author, and not necessarily that of the publisher.

Copyright © 2021 by Barbara Titus

All rights reserved. No part of this book may be reproduced, transmitted, or distributed in any form by any means, including, but not limited to, recording, photocopying, or taking screenshots of parts of the book, without prior written permission from the author or the publisher. Brief quotations for noncommercial purposes, such as book reviews, permitted by Fair Use of the U.S. Copyright Law, are allowed without written permissions, as long as such quotations do not cause damage to the book's commercial value. For permissions, write to the publisher, whose address is stated below.

Printed in the United States of America.

ISBN 978-1-955363-36-5 (Paperback)
ISBN 978-1-955363-37-2 (Digital)

Lettra Press books may be ordered through booksellers or by contacting:

Lettra Press LLC
30 N Gould St. Suite 4753
Sheridan, WY 828011
1 307-200-3414 | info@lettrapress.com
www.lettrapress.com

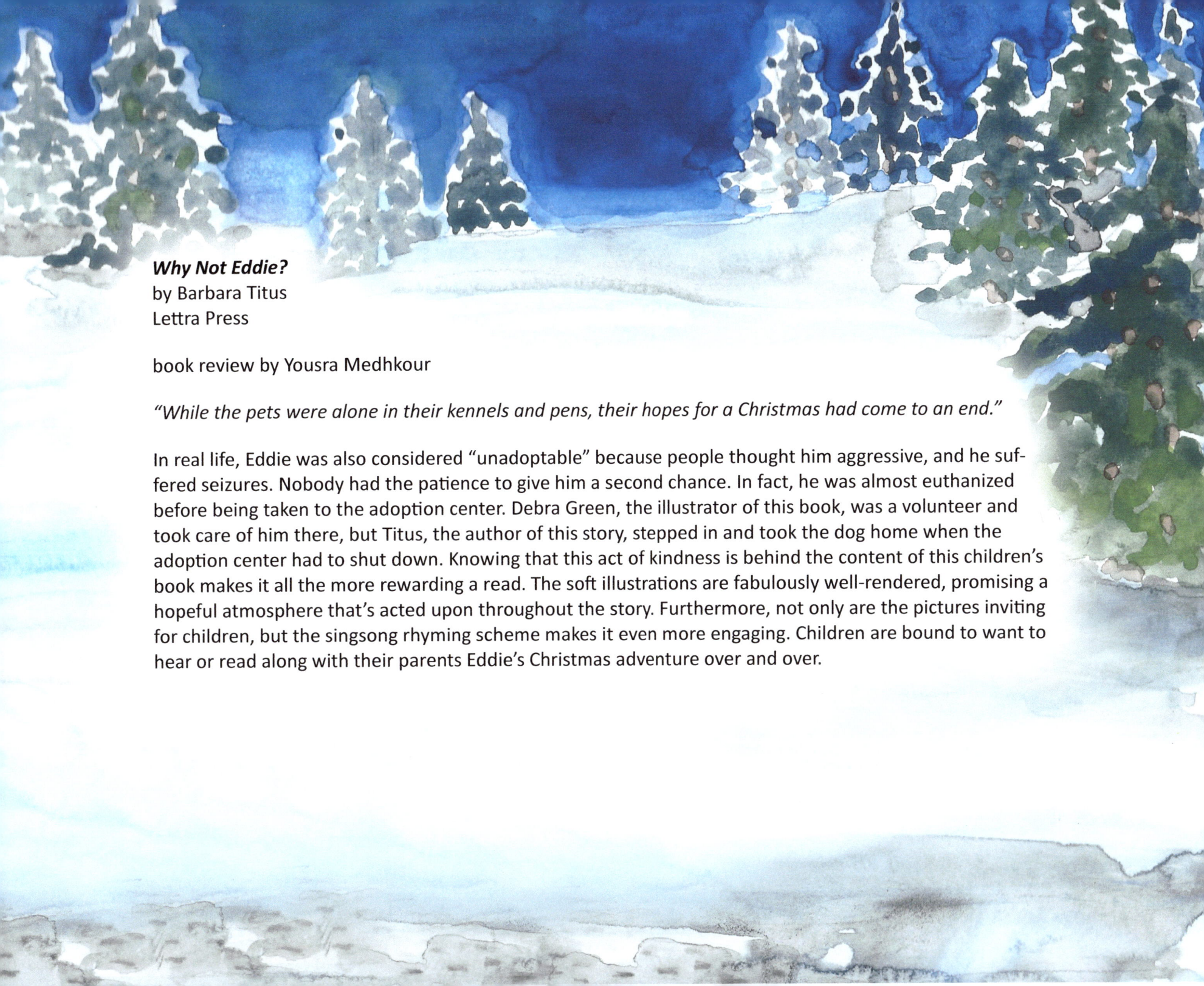

Why Not Eddie?
by Barbara Titus
Lettra Press

book review by Yousra Medhkour

"While the pets were alone in their kennels and pens, their hopes for a Christmas had come to an end."

In real life, Eddie was also considered "unadoptable" because people thought him aggressive, and he suffered seizures. Nobody had the patience to give him a second chance. In fact, he was almost euthanized before being taken to the adoption center. Debra Green, the illustrator of this book, was a volunteer and took care of him there, but Titus, the author of this story, stepped in and took the dog home when the adoption center had to shut down. Knowing that this act of kindness is behind the content of this children's book makes it all the more rewarding a read. The soft illustrations are fabulously well-rendered, promising a hopeful atmosphere that's acted upon throughout the story. Furthermore, not only are the pictures inviting for children, but the singsong rhyming scheme makes it even more engaging. Children are bound to want to hear or read along with their parents Eddie's Christmas adventure over and over.

Once one has lived with a wonderful dog, life without one is a life diminished (by Dean R. Koontz) To Eddie: My little buddy - my little man with four paws - who follows me everywhere and brings me so much joy. A person might wonder why I am dedicating a book to a dog. But Why not?

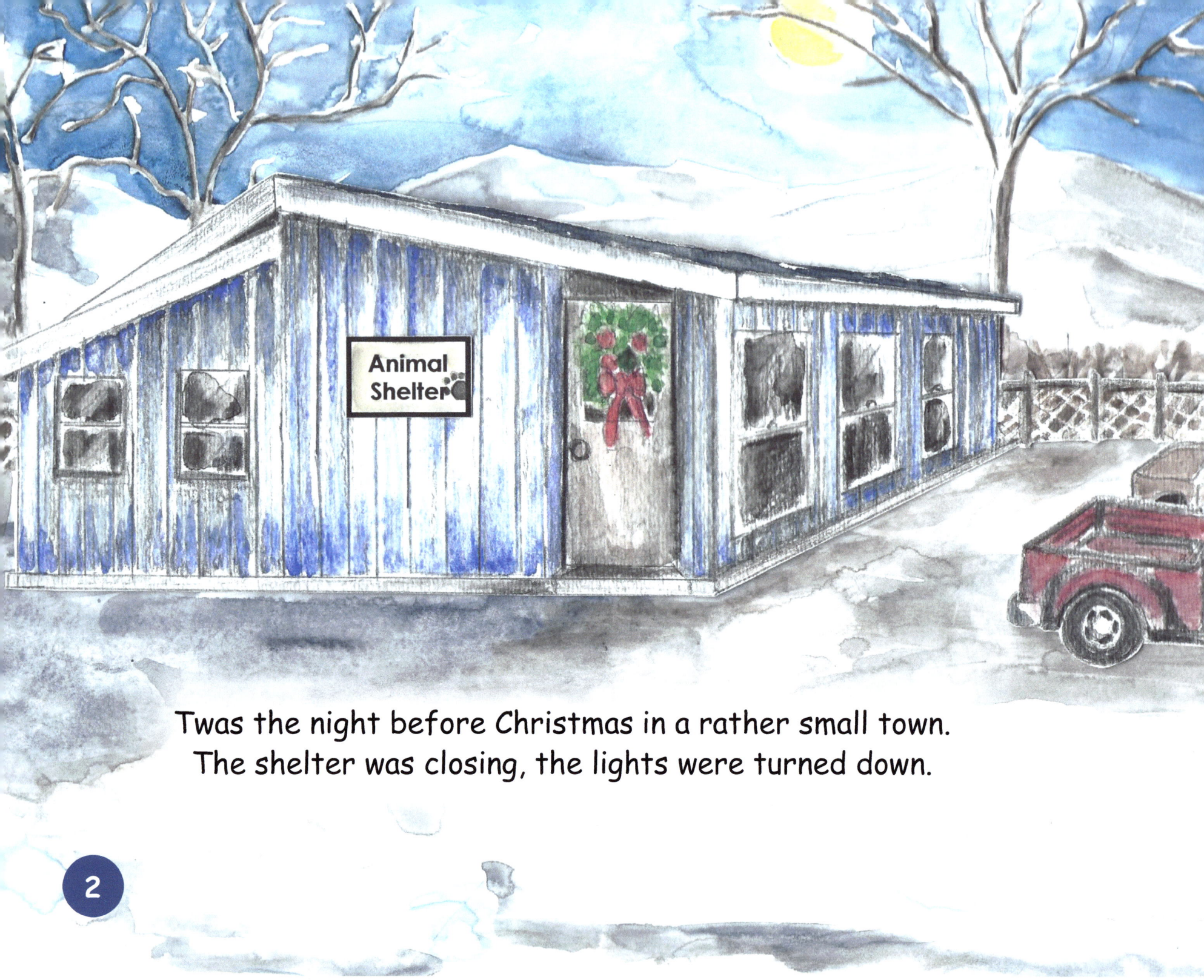

Twas the night before Christmas in a rather small town.
The shelter was closing, the lights were turned down.

The volunteers finished the last of their chores, and the last one to leave had locked the front door.

The pets had been fed and their bowls put away, The staff grabbed their keys; they were done for the day. Their voices were heard as they left for the night, "Merry Christmas, Merry Christmas!" as they drove out of sight.

While the pets were alone in their kennels and pens, their hopes for a Christmas had come to and end.

On that cold winter's eve the only sounds heard, were the puppies that whimpered and the kittens that purred.

Then out on the lawn came a bang and a clatter.
The dogs began barking, cats started to chatter.

Through the door he bounded and let out a loud shout; "It's Santa, wake up! I'll be letting you out! I've been 'round the world, my deliveries are done.! You'll be coming with me while the night is still young! I've a long list of families, still waiting for pets. I'm going to make this your best Christmas yet!"

"Katie wants Persians and a bunny for Jake, Jose wants Chihuahuas, and Pete wants a snake. Zach wants a pit bull, Troy wants a Setter. Liz wants a turtle, she sent me a letter!"

"There's a pig named Esther", there's Paulie the Parrot, a hen named Chicklet and Freddie the ferret. Let's go everyone! Come jump in the sleigh. I'll close this place up and we'll be on our way!

"But wait!" squawked Paulie, I just heard a bark! We forgot about Eddie, he's alone in the dark. He's back in the corner, he's alone and he's sad. He can't be adopted, they say he is bad!"

Santa returned to the kennels again, he found little Eddie alone in his pen. "I can't leave you here in this shelter alone. Naughty or not, you still need a home!"

They ran out to the sleigh and found it was packed. There wasn't much room, not even in the back. Rudolph was tired from the previous ride and kindly asked Santa to find a new guide. "With Rudolph too tired to show us the way, I must appoint someone to help guide the sleigh. Who will it be? We don't have much time, We have eight reindeer, we should have had nine!"

"NOT ME!" squealed Esther, "Me neither!" cried Freddie!! Squaaawk! Squaaawk! screamed Paulie! Why not choose Eddie?" So Eddie it was, up front in the sleigh, prepared for their journey, they went on their way.

Off they flew through the blizzards and snow. Each pet arrived safely adorned with a bow.

Beneath their trees and the twinkling lights, they peacefully, quietly, slept through the night.

The sleigh landed late on the North Pole lawn.

Santa climbed out with a stretch and a yawn. He was tired and ready for something to eat. They delivered the pets, now their job was complete.

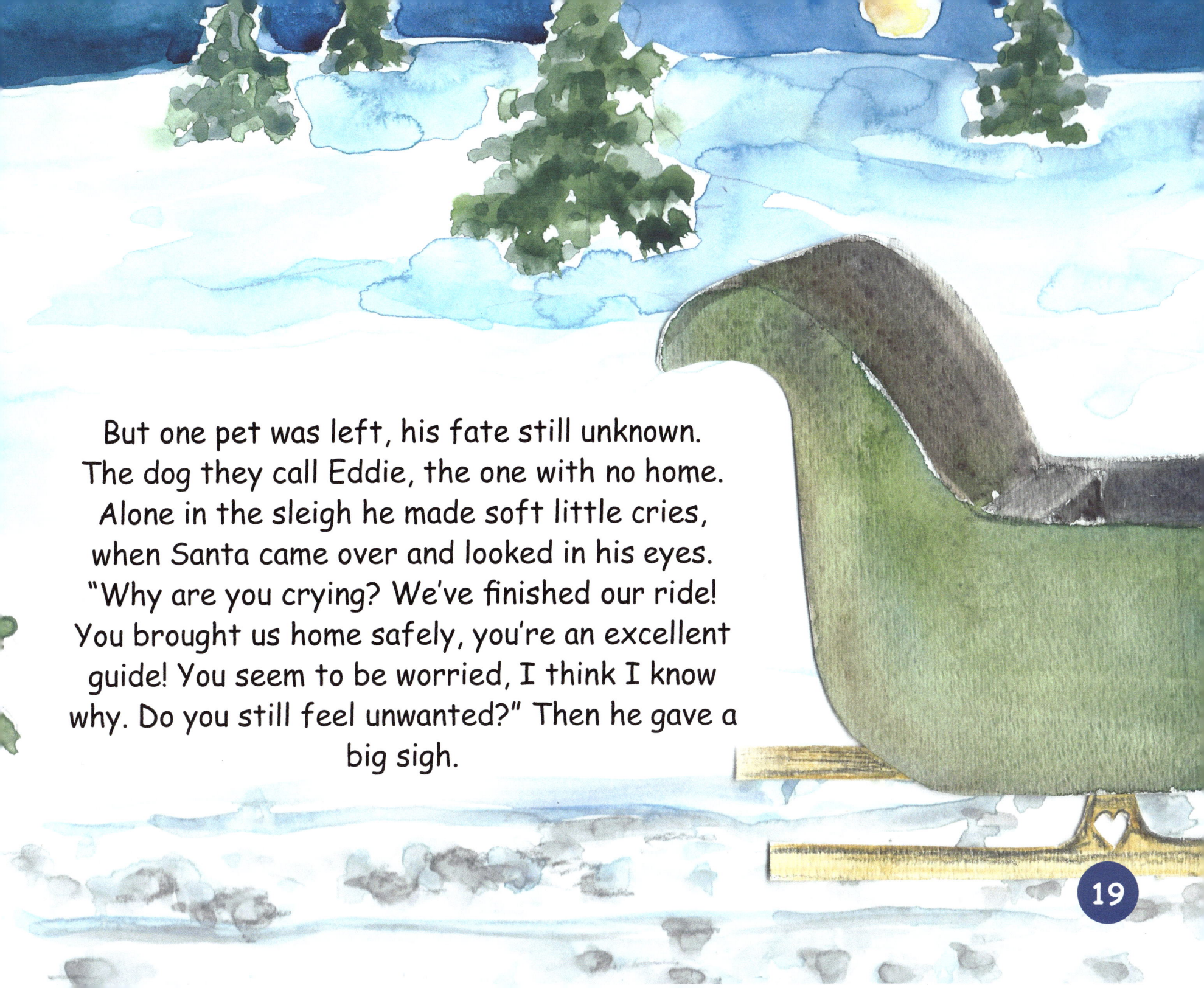

But one pet was left, his fate still unknown.
The dog they call Eddie, the one with no home.
Alone in the sleigh he made soft little cries,
when Santa came over and looked in his eyes.
"Why are you crying? We've finished our ride!
You brought us home safely, you're an excellent
guide! You seem to be worried, I think I know
why. Do you still feel unwanted?" Then he gave a
big sigh.

"We once had a dog, exactly your size. He had ears like you and those dark brown eyes. But soon he grew old, his life came to an end. Mrs. Clause still grieves, she misses her friend."

"So don't cry little dog, I've a plan you see. It's a secret tonight, between you and me." Then he hugged little Eddie and looked in his face; "Beneath our Christmas tree is where you'll be placed!"

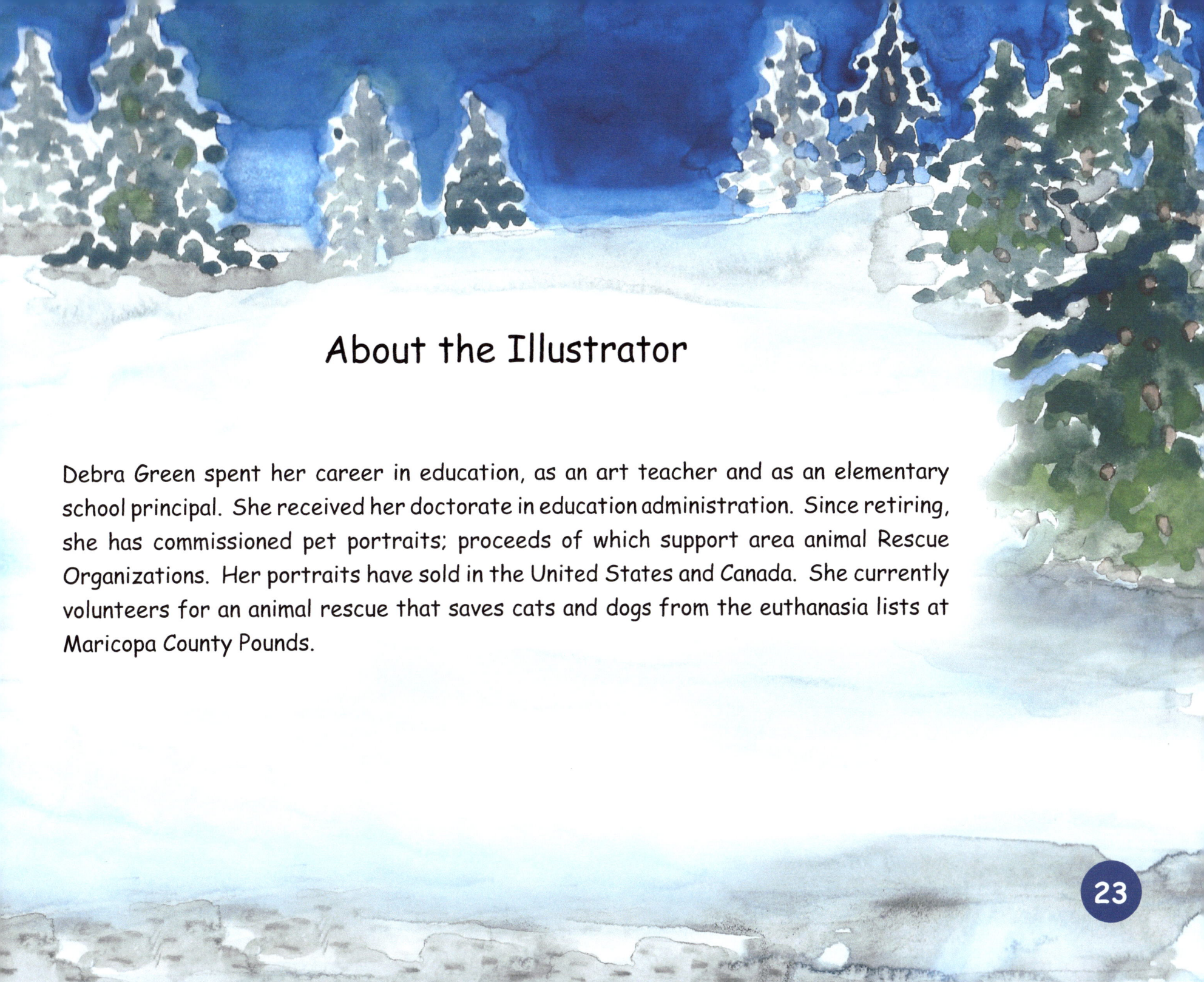

About the Illustrator

Debra Green spent her career in education, as an art teacher and as an elementary school principal. She received her doctorate in education administration. Since retiring, she has commissioned pet portraits; proceeds of which support area animal Rescue Organizations. Her portraits have sold in the United States and Canada. She currently volunteers for an animal rescue that saves cats and dogs from the euthanasia lists at Maricopa County Pounds.

ABOUT THE DOG

Eddie was on the list for euthanasia at the County Pound when he was rescued, then placed in an adoption center provided by Panacea Animal Welfare Sanctuary of Arizona. He was virtually unadoptable as his behavior was considered aggressive to those who had no desire to work with him or give him a second chance. He also had a medical history of seizures.

Almost a year later the adoption center had to close their doors. On that last day, there was only one pet left, the little dog named Eddie that no one wanted. I did what needed to be done and I volunteered to foster him. He was handed over to me from his friend Debra Green, another volunteer who knew him well and loved him as he was.

As a foster Mom I had a lot to learn about his personality and behavior. It didn't take long until we bonded. He became more and more comfortable in our home, accepting my husband and my other two pets.

Several weeks later I received a phone call from Debra wanting to know if I still had Eddie and how was he doing? I assured her he was doing just fine! She came to our home for a visit and our friendship began.

Eddie and I frequently hike in the Superstition Mountains of Arizona with Debra, her husband Larry and their two dogs (Tabby and Tad).

www.ingramcontent.com/pod-product-compliance
Lightning Source LLC
Chambersburg PA
CBHW041149070526
44579CB00004B/54